SURVIVING YOUR DEPOSITION

A Complete Guide to Help You Prepare For Your Deposition

• • • • • • •

Fredric J. Friedberg
Illustrated by Joy Friedberg

Schiffer Publishing Ltd®

4880 Lower Valley Road Atglen, pennsylvania 19310

Published by Schiffer Publishing Ltd.
4880 Lower Valley Road
Atglen, PA 19310
Phone: (610) 593-1777; Fax: (610) 593-2002
E-mail: Info@schifferbooks.com

For the largest selection of fine reference books on this and related subjects, please visit our web site at **www.schifferbooks.com**
We are always looking for people to write books on new and related
subjects. If you have an idea for a book please contact us at the above
address.

This book may be purchased from the publisher.
Include $3.95 for shipping.
Please try your bookstore first.
You may write for a free catalog.

In Europe, Schiffer books are distributed by
Bushwood Books
6 Marksbury Ave.
Kew Gardens
Surrey TW9 4JF England
Phone: 44 (0) 20 8392-8585; Fax: 44 (0) 20 8392-9876
E-mail: info@bushwoodbooks.co.uk
Website: www.bushwoodbooks.co.uk
Free postage in the U.K., Europe; air mail at cost.

Designed by Douglas Congdon-Martin
Type set in Zurich BT

Trade Edition ISBN: 978-0-7643-2681-3
Lawyer's Edition ISBN: 978-0-7643-2674-5

Written & Designed in the U.S.A.
Printed in China

CONTENTS

Introduction...7

How to Use This Guide...8

Chapter 1 – The Deposition Process...9

4

Chapter 2 – Ground Rules, Do's and Don'ts...57

The guide is not intended to serve as legal advice, but rather to prepare you for what you might expect during your deposition. This Guide may not cover every area of a deposition you may encounter. If you have any specific questions on the material covered in this guide you should contact an attorney.

INTRODUCTION

In May, 2004, after my book *The Illinois Watch: The Life and Times of a Great American Watch Company* was published, I had several lengthy discussions with its publisher, Peter Schiffer, on various aspects of litigation. Both his company, Schiffer Publishing, Ltd., as well as my employer, Toshiba America Medical Systems, Inc. were actively engaged in pending litigation as are many companies and individuals in today's society. We concluded that perhaps the most important and little known aspect of a lawsuit was the oral depositions that took place during the pre-trial discovery phase of a case. We agreed it was essential to explain and instruct witnesses on how to prepare and conduct themselves during a deposition. At his request, I have written this guide to help prepare prospective witnesses for their depositions. Being deposed is not a pleasant experience; it requires significant preparation and concentration and is frequently emotionally draining. However, using this book can help you be as prepared as possible to make the experience less threatening.

Please note that it is not the intent of this book to prepare a Federal Rule of Civil Procedure 30(b)(6) witness (a witness that is appearing in a representative capacity on a designated subject for a corporation) or for an expert witness, although virtually all of this guide is equally applicable to these witnesses as well.

I hope you enjoy the "Tales of the Transcript" that contain real life anecdotes from dozens of trial attorneys who have been kind enough to share them. There are also anecdotes excerpted from three legal humor books: "More Humor in the Court" (1994) edited by Mary Louise Gilman; "Disorderly Conduct" (1987) by Rodney R. Jones, Charles M. Sevilla and Gerald F. Uelman and "Disorder in the Court" (1992) by Charles M. Sevilla. They serve to reinforce much of the advice set forth in this book as well as to introduce some humor into this very serious subject.

Please note that in an effort for clarity, I have referred to lawyers as "he" or "him" rather than as "he/she" or "her" or "she." No chauvinism is intended; I merely thought it was best to use just one gender consistently throughout this guide.

HOW TO USE THIS GUIDE

To obtain the most value out of this guide and to maximize your preparation, first read the entire guide then go back and read only the shaded sections; then read only the sections with red letters and finally read the sections with green letters. Prior to your deposition, reread the red and green printed sections. If you have the time, read the entire guide again. For examples of the right and wrong way to reply, read the "Tales of the Transcript;" also, do so for some comic relief.

ACKNOWLEDGMENTS

I am grateful for the time and effort of John Chesney, Esq. of Philadelphia, Pennsylvania took from his busy trial schedule to review and provide his valuable comments and insights on my manuscript. Thanks also to my special assistant, Linda Daugherty, who again typed the drafts of this material on her own time. Lastly, and most importantly I am grateful as usual for my soul-mates' special contributions to my "projects," especially her superb original drawings. Thanks Joy.

THE DEPOSITION PROCESS

Chapter 1 – The Deposition Process

DISCOVERY

Unless a new lawsuit settles or is dismissed very quickly after it is first filed, the case will proceed to a set discovery period that is used to collect information. During "discovery" each side can seek information from the other in a variety of ways – by making requests to review documents and things, by asking them written questions called interrogatories that must be answered in writing and under oath, by requesting that the other side admit certain facts for purposes of the litigation, and by taking depositions, which involves asking witnesses questions to which they must respond under oath.

Documents are acquired by issuing a Request for Production or a "Notice to Produce." Beware you must not destroy any documents once you have received notice of a potential lawsuit that may relate to that document. This also includes electronic documents such as email. The topic of what documents must be preserved, what steps must be taken to preserve them, and when the duty to preserve a document arises is an extremely important one, but is not within the scope of this guide.

Information from individual persons is secured by using the **deposition process.** This is the single most powerful and important part of the discovery process and, in many instances, depositions represent the entire case, as so many cases settle prior to trial.

THE PURPOSE OF A DEPOSITION

Depositions are taken in a pending case for the following reasons and can be used in some of the following ways:

- To **gather facts and evidence.**

- To make a reasonable inquiry into any area that may **lead to admissible evidence**.

- To **narrow the issues**, stipulations (agreements) on facts and other matters can be made during your deposition that can shorten the trial.

- To **preserve testimony** that can be introduced at trial, in lieu of live testimony.

- To be **used at trial to "impeach" (contradict) a witness** if their story or answers changed from their deposition testimony. Opposing counsel will use it to try to trap you in a lie or omission at trial to establish that you are untruthful.

- To **refresh a witnesses' memory** while testifying at trial.

- To **eliminate surprise at trial**. Opposing counsel wants you to testify to a specific story so that you will repeat the exact story at trial. In this manner, they will know in advance what your story will be.

- To **prepare witnesses for trial.**

- To **assess the impression a witness** will make on a judge or jury. It may be important in evaluating your credibility as a witness and whether you will be believed by a judge or jury.

● ● ● ● ● ● ● ●

Tales of the Transcript

In November 1998, during the playing of portions of the video-taped deposition of Bill Gates, chairman of Microsoft, Inc., even the presiding federal judge over Microsoft's antitrust trial shook his head and laughed during portions of Bill Gates' deposition played in court because of his evasiveness and requested several times very basic words to be defined and many non-responses.

Obviously, the government lawyers surmised after Mr. Gates' deposition that this would serve to undermine Mr. Gates' credibility at trial and thereby strengthen the governments' case.

- To **persuade your opponent of the strengths of your case.**

- To **learn the weaknesses of your opponent's case.**

- To **limit the testimony of key adverse witnesses.**

- To **set up cross-examination on issues important to the trial.**

- To **plan trial strategy.**

- To **file "Summary Judgment" motions** – a procedure to request the judge to end the litigation without a trial; to do so you must prove that no factual issues are in dispute and the judge can render a decision by applying the law to the undisputed facts.

- To allow your deposition to be used by the other side opposing the Summary Judgment Motion.

- To **use at mediation and/or settlement conferences.**

- To allow the parties **to reach a settlement** once all the sides to the case are fully aware of all the relevant facts.

Tales of the Transcript

The governments' lawyers decided to play up Bill Gates's disastrous deposition, which played a central role in the trial. This deposition has been classified as a comic masterpiece of evasion and obfuscation. The transcript shows us a Gates who quibbles, truculently, with the meaning of words like "concerned," ask" and "very."

—Pride Before the Fall – The Trials of Bill Gates and the End of the Microsoft Era, John Heileman; New York; Harpers Collins Publishers, 2001.

THE IMPORTANCE OF A DEPOSITION

In light of the tremendous number of lawsuits (over 90%) that settle prior to trial, depositions are considered by many as the single-most powerful and important aspect of the pre-trial discovery process of a litigation. Therefore, to a great extent in many lawsuits, depositions actually serve in place of an actual trial. Depositions demonstrate the strengths of your claims or defenses and influence the settlement value of the litigation.

Because so many cases settle prior to trial, your deposition may be your only opportunity to testify. For this reason, good lawyers will prepare you as carefully for your deposition as they would for your trial testimony.

● ● ● ● ● ● ● ●

Tales of the Transcript

You have to be prepared for your deposition. You can usually never win a case based upon your deposition, but you can certainly lose it based on your replies.

Q: The charge here is theft of frozen chickens. Are you the defendant, sir?

A: No sir, I'm the guy who stole the chickens.

Disorderly Conduct, page 79.

At your deposition the questions you are asked will vary from predictable and fact-based to unexpected and hypothetical. You will be asked many probing questions, many seeking who, what, when, where, why, and was it written down? You may be asked to read many documents and then to interpret, explain, and comment on those documents. Your memory, judgment, and patience will be challenged and your concentration and goodwill will be stretched thin.

Your own lawyer's role during the process is limited. He may note objections that may later result in the question being disallowed at trial, but in most cases you will have to answer the question even if your lawyer objects. (For a discussion of the limited situations in which your lawyer may properly instruct you not to answer a question, please see at page 35). Your lawyer may ask you questions to help bring out additional relevant information that the opposing attorney may not pursue or to clarify an earlier point. However, your attorney's most important role is before your deposition to help you prepare. Once the deposition starts, you are largely on your own.*

The opposing attorney under our legal system does not objectively seek truth; his duty is to challenge and test as aggressively as necessary within the rules of procedure and ethics the version of the truth put forth by your side to the litigation. Therefore, opposing counsel will try many tactics and approaches to push you off your story and to get you to change your version of the facts and truth.

*Edward T. Wahl, "Are You Ready for Your Deposition?" 2005. faegre.com

ORAL TESTIMONY

At your deposition, you are referred to as the "deponent" or "witness" and you reply to oral questions from an attorney. Your replies (as well as any comment that is made in the room while the parties are "on the record") are recorded by a court reporter after you are sworn to tell the truth.

● ● ● ● ● ● ● ●

Tales of the Transcript

If you do not understand the question, say you do not understand the question and the examining attorney will revise the question so you understand. Do not be afraid to say you do not understand the question.

Q: All your responses must be oral, OK? What school did you go to?

A: Oral.

Q: How old are you?

A: Oral.

More Humor in the Courtroom, p. 32

DEPOSITION NOTICE

You are entitled to "reasonable" notice to attend your deposition. What is reasonable varies from jurisdiction to jurisdiction, depending on the laws and any special circumstances that may exist. However, in most instances less than ten days notice would not be viewed as reasonable. A non-party (that is, a person who is neither a plaintiff [the person or entity that initiates the lawsuit] nor a defendant [the person or entity that must defend the lawsuit] nor representatives of the parties) receives notice of his deposition by court order when he is served with a "Subpoena Re Deposition." This is a court order to appear. If you are a party to the case you will arrange with the other side when to appear, usually after receiving a "Notice of Deposition" delivered to your attorney, if the time called for in your Notice of Deposition is not convenient.

FAILURE TO APPEAR

If you fail to appear for your scheduled deposition, you can be "sanctioned" (punished) by a judge. This penalty can be a fine paid to the other side, or your claims or defenses could be dismissed if you are a party and you repeatedly fail to show up without good cause.

"My dog ate the subpoena!"

WHEN YOU SHOULD PROTEST THE SCHEDULING OF YOUR DEPOSITION

There are some legitimate reasons to try to protest, resist, or delay the scheduling of your deposition. These include:

- You are simply not available

- You are under criminal investigation and deposition could waive your rights against self-incrimination

- You are hospitalized or otherwise not medically competent to testify

- You are not mentally competent to testify

- You are under the effects of certain medication that would prevent your testifying accurately and reliably

- You have not had the necessary time to prepare fully for your deposition

- You are too young; i.e., you are a minor

- You are involved in a very serious business transaction that outweighs the importance of the deposition

- You are a senior executive of a significant organization, have no knowledge of the facts relevant to the lawsuit that could not be obtained from less senior personnel within the organization, and your business duties would be unreasonably interfered with if you were forced to attend.

The attorneys are usually readily agreeable to reschedule your deposition if the time set is inconvenient for you.

● ● ● ● ● ● ● ●

Tales of the Transcript

Always be as precise and concise as you can be in your replies.

Q: Doctor, did you say he was shot in the woods?

A: No, I said he was shot in the lumbar region.

GETTING OUT OF A DEPOSITION

As a non-party, you can sometimes get out of your deposition if you contact the lawyer that issued the subpoena and explain why you should not be involved or if you agree to meet to discuss what you know informally. If that occurs, be prepared to be asked by the other side to do the same.

● ● ● ● ● ● ● ●

Tales of the Transcript

When you reply to questions, you should try to not open up other areas of potential inquiry in your replies.

Q: Are you married?

A: No, I'm divorced.

Q: And what did your husband do before you divorced him?

A: A lot of things I didn't know about.

More Humor in the Court, p. 8.

As a general rule, a non-party witness cannot be required to travel more than 100 miles to be deposed. There is no similar restriction for party witnesses. Remember, a "party" to a case is either a named plaintiff or defendant. In the case of a representative deposition, in which an individual is designated to provide information on behalf of a corporation or other organization that is a party, the party taking the deposition will usually be required to take the deposition at a location close to the principal business offices of the entity being deposed.

As a non-party witness, you usually receive a check for $40.00 as a witness fee for your deposition.

● ● ● ● ● ● ● ●

Tales of the Transcript

There is no rule that says you have to make it easy for the opposing counsel. If he has to ask more questions to elicit the information he requires, it is all right to make him work to do so.

Q: What is your name?

A: Ernestine McDowell.

Q: And what is your marital status?

A: Fair.

More Humor in the Court, p. 6

LOCATION OF YOUR DEPOSITION

A deposition is typically taken in a conference room at the law offices of one of the attorneys involved in the case. Sometimes it can also take place in a hotel meeting room or even a lodging room, in a court reporter's office, or at the business office of one of the parties. Most parties do not like to have depositions in their business offices because the opposing parties might be able to roam into areas where they can see documents, overhear conversations, or strike up conversations with employees of the opposite side, and because it might appear unreasonable not to produce relevant documents, if they are requested during the deposition, that are located in the building where the deposition is taking place. The atmosphere at a deposition is often informal. Do not be fooled by this informality. If you state something wrong or inappropriate, you can harm your case.

● ● ● ● ● ● ● ●

Tales of the Transcript

As you will notice while reading the Tales of the Transcript in this guide, not all lawyers ask properly constructed and meaningful questions. But your job is to reply as briefly and accurately as you can and not to try to be humorous. Litigation is very serious business.

Q: Doctor, how many autopsies have you performed on dead people?

A: All my autopsies have been performed on dead people.

More Humor in the Court, p. 17

THOSE PRESENT AT YOUR DEPOSITION

Those present at a deposition are usually the parties to the case, the plaintiff and defendant, an attorney for each party, the witness, an attorney for the witness (unless the witness is being represented by an attorney for one of the parties) and a court reporter. A representative from an insurance company may be present if one of the parties is covered by an insurer. Occasionally, a legal assistant for an attorney may also attend. If required, an interpreter may attend. If the deposition is to be videotaped, then a videographer will be there. No judge is present to rule on objections or otherwise preside over the process, although judges will sometimes accept calls from the attorneys and rule on whether a question must be answered during the depositon.

You may not need an attorney present to represent you if you are not a party (non-party) to the lawsuit, but it is always prudent to have one with you if there is any possibility you may be implicated in the case or if you are a party to the case.

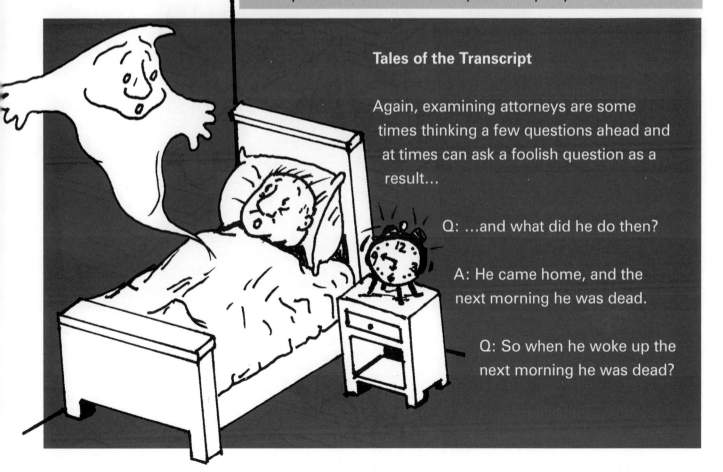

Tales of the Transcript

Again, examining attorneys are some times thinking a few questions ahead and at times can ask a foolish question as a result...

Q: ...and what did he do then?

A: He came home, and the next morning he was dead.

Q: So when he woke up the next morning he was dead?

DO NOT BRING A GUEST

As a general rule, do not bring anyone else to the deposition other than your lawyer. Your guests, under state rules, will usually not be allowed to sit in on the deposition and may end up waiting outside for a full day. Under Federal Rules, unlike at trial, there is no sequestration of witnesses at depositions, and, in fact, there are cases saying that, with the exception (oddly enough) of the press, pretty much anyone is in theory entitled to attend a deposition (not that most people would want to). In fact, owing to the non-sequestration rule, it is sometimes a good tactic to have a witness who is about to be deposed sit in on a deposition of someone who is being deposed.

● ● ● ● ● ● ● ●

Tales of the Transcript

Always make certain that you understand every word of every question before you reply. If you do not understand a word or question, say that you do not understand.

Q: Did you tell your lawyer that your husband had offered you indignities?

A: He didn't offer me nothing; he just said I could have the furniture.

More Humor in the Court, p. 7

DEPOSITION vs. TRIAL TESTIMONY

Testifying at a deposition is different than testifying at trial. The procedural rules during trial limit the lawyers to direct examination, cross-examination, and redirect examination. At a deposition, the deposing attorney is allowed broad latitude in terms of what he can ask about. For instance, he can ask you about hearsay (items you do not know about first-hand). Whether or not he can examine you by leading questions depends upon whether you are an adverse party or a witness who may fairly be deemed associated with an adverse party or otherwise "hostile" to the party taking the deposition.

Hearsay is permitted in depositions, unlike in a court room. If you have the information sought you have to reveal it even if you only learned it from someone else. However, some lawyers may request that you reply only if you have "personal knowledge" of a matter. For example, during your deposition you can be asked what your boss told you about why he fired your co-worker or what you heard about it from others. When responding, make it clear whether you are providing first-hand knowledge or second-hand information and only answer the question asked. For instance, if the question is "What did your boss tell you?" and she told you nothing, the answer is "Nothing," not "She didn't say anything, but another supervisor told me…"

If your testimony describes conversations, identify whether you are paraphrasing or quoting precise conversations of others.

Tales of the Transcript

I once prepared a witness to be careful about not testifying as to what was in someone else's mind when they made a statement to him. In the deposition, he was asked what another person meant by a statement to the witness made during a conversation, the witness responded "I could not read his mind…over the telephone."

Courtesy of Barry Heller, Esq.

REQUEST FOR DOCUMENTS

As a party to a lawsuit you may receive, in addition to their "Notice Re Deposition," a separate "Request for Production of Documents." As a non-party you will receive a "Subpoena Duces Tecum" if you are required to produce records.

Tales of the Transcript

Again, there is no harm in making the lawyer deposing you work for his answers.

Q: Could you see him from where you were standing?

A: I could see his head.

Q: And where was his head?

A: Just above his shoulders.

More Humor in the Court, p. 45

You are likely to be shown several documents during your deposition; you will be given these documents for several objectives:

> • To **authenticate the document**; to establish that the document is what it appears to be.
> • To **establish that you have personal knowledge regarding the document** or the information in the document.
> • To **learn all you know regarding the preparation, transmittal and receipt of the document.**
> • To **learn all you know regarding the information in the document.**

Before answering any questions concerning any document, you should do the following:

> • Look at the document to see who wrote it, who it was sent to, who else received copies of the document, and whether you recognize it as a document you have seen before.
> • If the document contains handwritten notes, check the notes to determine whether they are in your handwriting or whether the notes were directed to you.
> • Look at major subheadings on the document to help you determine if you have seen this document before.
> • If you have never seen the document, return it to the attorney. Advise him that you do not recall ever having seen this document. Only read the document in detail if the attorney then asks you to read it.

If you are subpoenaed or instructed to produce documents at your deposition, bring three copies of each document: one for yourself, one for your lawyer and one for the opposing counsel. Also bring the originals in case there is a dispute as to the accuracy of the copies. If you are represented by counsel, give the originals to your lawyer and he will arrange to give copies of them to the other side.

Tales of the Transcript

Even some of the brightest and most successful executives can damage their credibility by how they conduct themselves during their depositions.

In a rambling 50-minute video segment pulled from Bill Gates's three-day deposition in a 1998 antitrust suit against Microsoft, Gates engaged in a verbal duel with U.S Justice Department attorney David Boies, splitting hairs over literal interpretations of e-mails, memos and words such as "compete," "concerned," "ask," and "very" and refusing to concede that company officials focused their efforts primarily on Netscape.

Boies confronted Gates with an e-mail the Microsoft chairman wrote to a subordinate on January 5, 1996, that said in part, "Winning internet browser share is a very, very important goal for us." Gates said he didn't remember writing that specifically. But Boies pressed him about what companies he would include in the term browser share.

"There's no companies included in that," Gates responded.

"Well, if you're winning browser share, that must mean that some other company is producing browsers and you're comparing your share of browsers with somebody else's share of browsers," Boies replied. "Is that not so, sir?"

"I'm very confused about what you're asking," Gates replied. After Boies rephrased his question, Gates played the artful dodger. "It doesn't appear I'm talking about any other companies in that sentence," he replied coyly.

While the tape was being played at the trial, however, all eyes were on U.S. District Court Judge Thomas Penfield Jackson, who audibly laughed and shook his head during the sometimes comical war of words between the argumentative attorney and the hostile witness.

At the conclusion of the playing of the Gates deposition segment, Jackson asked, "How long did the deposition take?"

"Three days," Boies responded, implying that it was due to Gates being evasive to the point of appearing confused.

Gates had been shown a document sent to him by Brad Chase, a Microsoft V.P., on March 13, 1997, that said, "We need to continue our jihad next year...Browser share needs to remain a key priority for our field and marketing efforts."

"It doesn't say Microsoft," Gates said in his deposition.

"Well," said Boies, "when it says 'we' there, do you understand that means something other than Microsoft sir?"

"It could mean Brad Chase's group," Gates replied.

Gates was more forthcoming when asked what Chase meant by 'jihad.' "I think he is referring to our vigorous efforts to make a superior product and to market that product," Gates said.

Some of the exchanges evoked laughter in the courtroom. Boies quizzed Gates about what "non-Microsoft" browsers he was concerned about when he e-mailed about them in January 1996.

Gates said he was confused. "I'm sure – what's the question? Is it – are you asking me about when I wrote this e-mail or what are your asking me about?"

Said Boies, "I'm asking you about January of 1996."

Replied Gates: "That month?"

Said Boies: "Yes, sir?"

Replied Gates: "And what about it?"

DATES ON DOCUMENTS

Beware not to interpret a date shown on a document as being the true date of its writing. If you do not recall the date the document was prepared, do not testify that the date on the document is accurate. **Some computer programs automatically change the date a document was created to the date it is printed or sent.**

● ● ● ● ● ● ● ●

Tales of the Transcript

Do not embellish your answer. When a simple "no" will suffice, say "no" and keep quiet.

Q: Do you drink when you're on duty?

A: I don't drink when I'm on duty, unless I come on duty drunk.

More Humor in the Court, p. 48

The Federal rules limit the duration of depositions "to one day of seven hours." This time can be extended by agreement of the parties or by court order. If the parties have agreed that a non-party's deposition may continue for more than seven hours, the non-party will be required to obtain a protective order from the court if he wishes to limit his deposition to seven hours.

● ● ● ● ● ● ● ●

Tales of the Transcript

Again answer as briefly as you can. Do not embellish your replies. If you can answer "yes" or "no" simply do so.

Q: Are you sexually active?

A: No, I just lie there.

RECESSES OR BREAKS

Generally, you can request a brief recess at any time during your deposition to stretch your legs, to get refreshed, to use the bathroom, if you are tired or become angry or frustrated, etc. However, the Federal rules state that your lawyer is not to confer with you and cannot take a recess while a question is pending except to determine whether a legal privilege (see page 41) should be asserted. You should be aware that in some federal jurisdictions (and in some states, too) discussions you may have with your lawyer during breaks in your depositon will not be considered privileged, and the other side will be able to inquire into the content of such discussions. Even, in those jurisdictions, however, you will ordinarily be able to have a privileged discussion with your lawyer about whether information being sought in your deposition is itself privileged.

If the number of breaks become excessive, the other lawyer may complain and start to refuse the request if you are breaking his rhythm or otherwise disrupting him.

Remember that many experienced lawyers expect you to be tired and worn down by the end of the day and wait until then to pose important questions or right before lunch break. Under the Federal rules, if you are too tired to continue, you

can "call it a day" and ask for the deposition to end. You will then have to agree to have it completed on another day. Generally, if you tell the opposing lawyer that you are too tired to give testimony that can be relied upon, he will agree to terminate the session and complete your deposition at a later date.

LET'S TAKE A Break

In addition to helping you prepare for your deposition, your lawyer could:

• Protect you from abusive tactics;

• Object to improper questions

• Help clarify the record and your story by asking you questions at the end of your deposition.

A party to a case should always be represented by an attorney. A non-party may attend without a lawyer unless he runs the risk of being implicated in the case. In some cases, non-parties, such as former employees of a party, may choose to be represented by the lawyer for the party for whom they formerly worked.

●　●　●　●　●　●　●　●

Tales of the Transcript

Make certain you understand every word in the question before you reply. If you do not understand a word, ask for it to be defined.

Q: The truth of the matter is that you were not an unbiased, objective witness, isn't it? You too were shot in the fracas?

A: No, sir. I was shot midway between the fracas and the navel.

34

OBJECTIONS

Unlike a courtroom trial, objections are generally few in a deposition and in any event there is no judge to rule on them at your deposition. So unless you are specifically instructed by your attorney not to answer, you will usually have to reply. Some disputes concerning objections may be taken up immediately with the judge via phone if they are important; at other times they may go to a special magistrate to handle such disputes, either immediately or at a later date. It is not unusual for lawyers to argue during your deposition over what may or may not be a proper question or area of inquiry.

● ● ● ● ● ● ● ●

Tales of the Transcript

My company was involved in a very contemptuous lawsuit over several years. As frequently happens, the opposing lawyers end up hating each other and become very confrontational. During one of the depositions with our vice president and CFO, our lawyer refused to let our CFO reply to a question and the other lawyer became enraged and reached for the phone to call the judge. (This was during the time cell phone were not in regular use yet). As we were paying for the hotel conference room, our lawyer reached over and grabbed the phone out of his hands and told him to find his own phone to use. After about thirty minutes the lawyers calmed down sufficiently for the deposition to continue.

OBJECTIONS AS TO THE SUBSTANCE OF THE QUESTION

Your lawyer must make a timely objection to the substance of a question with an appropriate instruction not to answer if the question involves:

- A privileged communication (please see page 41)

- Attorney's Work Product – work done by your attorney in preparation for the litigation

- Certain confidential information

- Trade secrets

- In some courts, information sought that can have no possible bearing on the issues in the case

Your lawyer must also object:

- To enforce a limitation on discovery previously imposed by the judge

- To prepare to suspend your deposition to seek a protective (confidential) order from the judge

Some courts have ruled that a witness may refuse to answer only questions that call for privileged information, and that you must answer all other questions subject to your attorney's objection. If the attorneys fight over this issue during your deposition, your lawyer can terminate the deposition and go to court to obtain a protective (confidentiality) order or "certify the question." If your attorney instructs you to not answer and the opposing counsel insists on getting a reply, he may tell the court reporter to "certify the question" which means he intends to have you appear in court in front of a judge to instruct you to reply to the question.

The Federal rules are explicit on the point that you can refuse to answer only in three circumstances: (1) to protect privilege; (2) to enforce previous limitations on discovery set by the judge, and (3) to suspend examination in order to seek a protective order. (i.e., protecting work product, trade secrets, preventing harassment through grossly improper questioning, etc.).

If a judge orders you to reply to a question, you will be well-advised to answer or face serious consequences. If you do not answer you will be in contempt of court and the judge could fine you or sentence you to jail time. If you are a party to the case, the judge could even dismiss your case or enter a judgment against you (or more likely in the case of a single refusal to provide information) could rule that you will not be allowed to challenge the other side's evidence on the relevant issue or that the issue will be deemed to have been proved against you for purposes of trial.

If you are unsure if a question might reveal a privilege you may consult with your lawyer to determine if your reply would disclose privileged information.

● ● ● ● ● ● ● ●

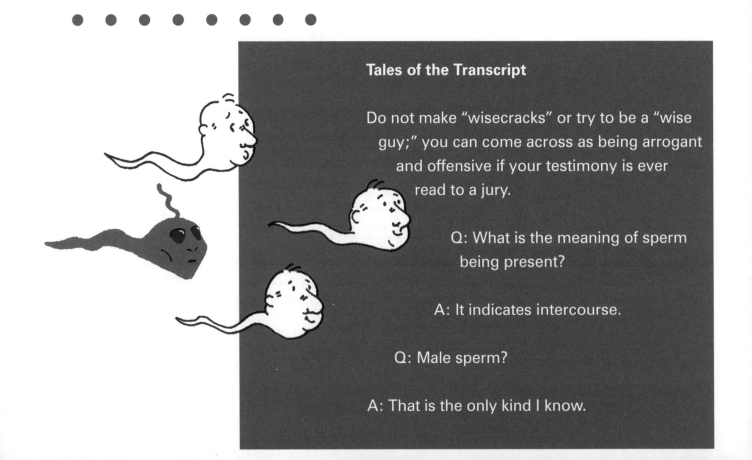

Tales of the Transcript

Do not make "wisecracks" or try to be a "wise guy;" you can come across as being arrogant and offensive if your testimony is ever read to a jury.

Q: What is the meaning of sperm being present?

A: It indicates intercourse.

Q: Male sperm?

A: That is the only kind I know.

COMMON OBJECTIONS

The most common objections to deposition questions are:

- Question was asked and answered

- Ambiguous

- Compound question

- Form of question

- Requests privileged information

- Argumentative

- Calls for speculation, guess or conjecture

- Assumes an untrue fact

- Assumes facts not in evidence

- Confusing

- Unintelligible

- Hypothetical improper question

- Misquotes witnesses' testimony

- Mischaracterizes the witnesses' testimony

- Narrative answer requested

- Overly broad, vague or indefinite

- Speech, rather than a question

- Unfair summary of testimony

- Requires witness' substantive interpretation of key terms

- Lack of foundation

Under the Federal rules, most lawyers and most judges agree that an attorney may specify the basis for his objection to a question. For example, in addition to stating that he objects to the "form of the question," your lawyer will ordinarily be able to state the basis of his objection to form – such as, that the question is "compound" or "asked and answered," etc. Some jurisdictions do not allow the lawyer to say anything other than "objection to the form of the question," but most courts recognize that this rule runs counter to the principle of the Federal rules that objections that could have been "obviated" by timely objection will be waived if not cured at the deposition. In other words, most courts recognize that it is proper to let the other lawyer know that his question was "ambiguous" or "assumed facts not in evidence" and the like. The Federal rules do, however, make "speaking" objections improper. "Speaking" objections are basically objections that seek to coach the witness as how to reply.

Pay close attention if your lawyer objects to the "form of a question"; it is many times a tip to you that he does not like the question and/or you should be very careful in answering. Keep in mind the objections noted above and listen for any reason your attorney states that the question is inappropriate; it will tip you off as to what to be on the lookout for. Frequently, the objections of your counsel will provide you with information that will help you determine the appropriate reply. For example, if he objects stating "asked and answered" you can reply that you already answered that question. If he objects "calls for speculation" you can state I cannot answer without guessing. A good lawyer will provide many subtle and direct and indirect warnings and instructions to you via his objections and dialogue with opposing counsel, so please listen to them carefully.

Remember objections by your lawyer serves two purposes: (1) to preserve the record so a judge can rule on it later, and (2) to provide a "cue" to you that there is something to be alert to in the question or some problem with the question.

Tales of the Transcript

Make certain you understand the advice of your lawyer. If you do not understand make him explain information so you do understand it.

Q: Do you think this girl was raped, in your heart?

A: I've got mixed feelings about it.

Q: Then why did you plead guilty?

A: Well, my lawyer said that was the best thing for me to do.

Q: What do you think of your lawyer?

A: Well, I've got mixed feelings about him, also.

More Humor in the Court, p. 149

OBJECTION TO CONDUCT OF COUNSEL

Your attorney may place on the record objections to the opposing counsels' conduct for the following type of behavior:

- Being overly disparaging to you or your counsel

- Being overly hostile to you or your counsel

- Being obnoxious

- Being offensive

- Harassing

- Misleading or intentionally trying to confuse you (by misstating facts, evidence, dates, etc.)

- Rushing your replies

- Interrupting or cutting off your replies

● ● ● ● ● ● ● ●

Tales of the Transcript

Your replies during your deposition can sink your case if you are not careful.

Q: Are you sure you did not enter the Seven-Eleven on 40th and N.E. Broadway and hold up the cashier on June 17th of this year?

A: I'm pretty sure.

Disorderly Conduct, page 84

PRIVILEGED COMMUNICATIONS

You are not required to testify about discussions that are protected by legal privilege. These are:

- Attorney/Client Communications

- Husband/Wife Communications

- Doctor/Patient Communications

- Penitential Communications between clergy and congregant

- Psychotherapy-patient communications, mental health professionals, rape counselors, domestic violence counselors, etc.

Other privileges:

- Attorney "Work Product" – you are not required to turn over to the other side work that your attorney has produced to prepare to handle and represent you in the litigation or that contain his trial or litigation strategy. Note, however, that if you use work product material (or privileged material) to refresh your recollections in preparing for your deposition and it, in fact, refreshes your recollection on a matter on which you are examined, that material may become discoverable by the other side.

- Privilege Against Self Incrimination – under the Fifth Amendment of the United States Constitution you can refuse to reply to a question you reasonable believe may help to prove you have engaged in a criminal activity.

Do not disclose privileged information during your deposition; it could result in serious damage to your case.

In a very few jurisdictions, certain other privileged relationships are protected. These are:

- Parent/child communications

- Ombudsman/grievant in certain business situations

- Consultant/client communications

● ● ● ● ● ● ● ●

Tales of the Transcript

If you are not truthful in your replies, it could end up cost-
ing you your case.

During President Clinton's deposition in the Paula Jones
sexual harassment lawsuit, the following personal inter-
change took place:

Q: Did you have an extramarital sexual affair with Monica
Lewinsky?

A: No.

Q: If she told someone that she had a sexual affair with
you beginning in November of 1995, would that be a lie?

A: It's certainly not the truth. It would not be the truth.

Q: I think I used the term "sexual affair." And so the record
in completely clear, have you ever had sexual relations
with Monica Lewinsky, as that term is defined in Deposition Exhibit 1, as modified by the Court.

A: I have never had sexual relations with Monica Lewinsky.
I've never had an affair with her.

Almost every depositions has some of the following personal questions that you should be prepared to answer, such as:

- Age

- Educational background

- Be prepared to acknowledge employment gaps if you have any so they are not made a big issue

- Employment history (going back at least 10 years)

- Why you left a certain job; whether leaving was your choice of your employer's

- Marital status and history

- Religious affiliation

- Family and personal income in some cases

- Driving records in some cases

- Medication or drugs you have taken (now?)

- Previous depositions– when and what kind of case(s)

- Previous lawsuits

- Any arrests or criminal convictions

- Previous involvement in a litigation

In a personal injury case, be prepared to:

- List all of your injuries, from your head to your feet, including psychological trauma, sleep disorders, etc.

• List all medical treatment received before and after the incident

• List all activities you cannot do now or have limitations doing now, that you used to do before the incident

• List how the injuries impact your routine daily activities, sports, relationships, recreation, work, etc.

• Show physical signs of your injury or scars to the other side

• List all time you lost from work, wages lost, and all medical costs

The Federal rules protect you from answering questions that cause "annoyance, embarrassment, oppression or undue burden or expense." Therefore, you do not have to reply to questions that are not germane to the case in dispute. However, your attorney should be notified if there is anything in your personal history that may be an area of concern, such as a criminal record. This could impact your credibility. So both you and your attorney should be prepared to deal with it.

● ● ● ● ● ● ● ●

Tales of the Transcript

This is an example of a precise reply:

Q: What is your date of birth?

A: July fifteenth.

Q: What year?

A: Every year.

Familiarize yourself with your medical records if the nature of your case may involve your medical history. These records usually provide opposing counsel with a treasure trove of material for questions; so be prepared to know the details so you can testify accurately. Make certain your lawyer is fully knowledgeable about your prior medical conditions and history as the opposite side will be, especially if there is a lawyer present representing an insurance carrier.

Tales of the Transcript

Sometimes you have to respond to a non-intelligent question. The examining lawyer is bound to have some lapses or poor questions during the course of your deposition. Usually, a lawyer would say "strike that" immediately to the court reporter once he realized that he had made a mistake or asked an errant question.

Q: What happened then?

A: He told me, he says, "I have to kill you because you can identify me."

Q: Did he kill you?

A: No.

More Humor in the Court, p. 26

DO NOT BRING NOTES OR DOCUMENTS
TO YOUR DEPOSITION

Unless you have first reviewed your notes or documents with your lawyer, do not bring any notes or documents to your deposition. Any material that you refer to in your deposition, use to prepare for it or to refresh your recollection, will likely be required to be produced to the other side. Beware that instructions from your lawyer and legal strategy documents must not be brought with you or discussed during your deposition. If you do so, you can lose the protection of the attorney/client privilege. Your lawyer should remind you prior to your deposition not to bring any material of this nature to your deposition.

● ● ● ● ● ● ● ●

Tales of the Transcript

Beware that electronic communications are no different than any other correspondence and are subject to production during a lawsuit and you can be questioned about them.

Q: Did you correspond with the plaintiff at any time?

A: No, I just sent him a few emails.

You should ask your counsel to find out the demeanor of the opposing lawyer as well as his approach to questioning. Some lawyers will methodically proceed step by step in an orderly sequence; others will leap-frog from topic to topic in no set sequence; others may cut right to the chase and ask you flat out at the beginning of the case "What did my client do wrong?" "Why did you continue to market a product you knew was defective?"

The attorney asking you questions will usually be "nice" or "hostile." A nice lawyer wants you to be comfortable and relaxed so you let your defenses down. Then they will try to shake you up by becoming increasingly nasty and hostile.

A hostile attorney starts off being nasty, trying to get you to fall apart and reveal damaging information. They try to test you "under fire" to see how you would stand up at trial.

In both instances, this is an act. You should remain calm, polite, and respectful. There is no right or wrong way to conduct a deposition or to examine a witness. Every lawyer's style differs and they generally adjust to the nature of the witness and the case.

SIDE BARS

Don't be afraid to ask to speak with your attorney. **Your attorney is with you to help you. There is nothing wrong with
asking to stop the deposition so you can speak with your
attorney for a moment, as long as you limit it to a reasonable number of times. If you were to do this too often, the
opposing counsel will protest this tactic. Again, if you are
thoroughly prepared hopefully there will be no surprises or
unanticipated areas of inquiry.** Beware neither you nor your
attorney can request a break while a question is pending unless it involves an area that is privileged. Also, as noted earlier, make sure you know whether these discussions will, in the
jurisdiction in question, be privileged, as the answer to that
question may determine what you will and will not wish to
discuss with your attorney (and what he will and will not want
you to discuss with him) during deposition breaks. Generally,
it is always appropriate to let your lawyer know if you believe
you have provided inaccurate testimony in the preceding part
of a deposition.

● ● ● ● ● ● ● ●

Tales of the Transcript

Again, certain replies can severely harm your case, so pause before
you reply and carefully consider how you will respond.

Q: What doctor treated you for the injuries you sustained while at
work?

A: Dr. J.

Q: And what kind of physician is Dr. J?

A: Well, I'm not sure, but I remember that you said he was a good
plaintiff's doctor!

Disorderly Conduct, page 107

MEET WITH YOUR LAWYER EARLY

As soon as you know you must be deposed, meet with your lawyer, learn the details of the case, what your role and areas of the inquiry are likely to be, review all relevant documents and court papers and practice questions and answers with your lawyer over and over.

RELATED DEPOSITIONS

There could be dozens of depositions taken in a single litigation. You should make certain that your lawyer lets you read any other deposition from the case that may become a subject of inquiry during your deposition. A good lawyer should have as part of his "Attorney Work Product" loose-leaf binders prepared containing each document, exhibit or deposition transcript that involves you and that you may be questioned about. This binder should include all relevant email, personal calendars, telephone messages/logs, personal notes, notes you may have written on documents, etc., anything you may be questioned about.

● ● ● ● ● ● ● ●

Tales of the Transcript

This is funny, but a simple "yes" reply would have been sufficient.

Q: Are you qualified to give a urine sample?

A: Yes, I have been since early childhood.

Your lawyer must get you fully prepared to handle your deposition. This includes:

• Meetings and interviews with you concerning the causes of action in the case and your role in the proceeding.

• Complete review and questioning concerning the documents in your witness binder.

• Practice questions you will encounter, especially in the most critical areas of your likely testimony. A good lawyer will propose practice questions and replies over and over again with you until you are comfortable and will make a strong and affirmative witness.

• You should read this guide "Surviving Your Deposition" during your preparation and just prior to your deposition.

• Allow as much time as is required to prepare for your deposition, be it hours, days or weeks.

• If you are called to provide a deposition, your participation is mandatory, so rely on your lawyer, this guideline and do your best.

• Remember there is no substitute for preparation. The key to a good deposition is preparation, preparation, preparation...

Tales of the Transcript

President Clinton, in the Paula Jones sexual harassment lawsuit, should have been prepared to reply to the following questions:

Q: At any time were you and Monica Lewinsky alone together in the Oval Office?

A: I don't recall, but as I said, when she worked at the legislative affairs office, they always had somebody there on the weekends. I typically worked some on the weekends. Sometimes they'd bring me things on the weekends. She – it seems to me she brought things to me once or twice on the weekends. In that case, whatever time she would be in there, drop it off, exchange a few words and go, she was there. I don't have any specific recollections of what the issues were, what was going on, but when the Congress is there, we're working all the time, and typically I would do some work on one of the days of the weekends in the afternoon.

Q: So I understand, your testimony is that it was possible, then, that you were alone with her, but you have no specific recollection of that ever happening?

A: Yes, that's correct. It's possible that she, in, while she was working there, she was the only person there. That's possible.

Q: Have you ever met with Monica Lewinsky in the White House between the hours of midnight and six a.m.?

A: I certainly don't think so.

Q: Have you ever met –

A: Now, let me just say, when she was working there, during, there may have been a time when we were all – we were up working late. There are lots of, on any given night, when the Congress is in session there are always several people around until late in the night, but I don't have any memory of that. I just can't say that there could have been a time when that occurred, I just – but I don't remember it.

Q: Certainly if it happened, nothing remarkable would have occurred?

A: No, nothing remarkable. I don't remember it.

Occasionally, especially in a major litigation, a party may be required to give more than one deposition, but this will be unusual.

● ● ● ● ● ● ● ●

Tales of the Transcript

Listen to the question carefully; if you understand it, reply concisely and accurately.

Q: Mr. Guzman, can you read and write and understand the English language?

A: Si.

Disorderly Conduct, page 108.

YOUR DEPOSITION CAN ONLY HURT YOU

There are many reasons to take a deposition. However, it is not taken to exonerate the person being deposed. Simply put, your deposition can only hurt you or your company.*

Your role is basically to play defense, to avoid damaging your case. Resist the urge to swing for the fences to try to hit a game winning home run. You will very likely not succeed in any event.

If there is a "bad" or "awkward" fact, let your lawyer deal with it. Your job is to be concise, answer truthfully, not volunteer information, and not budge from your testimony, position, views that you believe to be truthful.

● ● ● ● ● ● ● ●

Tales of the Transcript

Be careful the answer you give does not damage your case.

Q: Tell me in your own words why you reached in his pocket and took out the bill-fold?

A: Something to do, I guess, sir.

More Humor in the Court, p. 55

---

*Robert F. Tyson, Jr., "How to Successfully Testify at Your Deposition." *Journal of Financial Planning,* 1998.

Practice your deposition skills. Have your attorney drill you with sample questions and critique your performance. Practice listening to each question, thinking about and analyzing your answer, and delivering it properly. Do not assume that answering deposition questions is easy. You will be facing a skilled interrogator, perhaps for as long as seven hours a day.

● ● ● ● ● ● ● ●

Tales of the Transcript

Even answer the silly questions politely and accurately.

Q: Were you present when your picture was taken?

Disorder in the Court, p. 64

Q: Was that the same nose you broke as a child?

More Humor in the Court, p. 27

Q: How far from the chair were you when it hit you?

More Humor in the Court, p. 28

Q: At the time you first saw Dr. McCarty, had you ever seen him prior to that time?

More Humor in the Court, p. 28

GROUND RULES, DO'S & DON'TS

Chapter 2 – Ground Rules, Do's and Don'ts

At the outset of your deposition, the opposing attorney will usually explain to you the ground rules of a deposition. These are also called "admonitions." You should understand these ground rules before opposing counsel explains them to you so you will feel more comfortable and in control. The usual admonitions are set forth below; following each explanation, the attorney will ask if you understand them.

• The **oath** you have been given is the same oath that would be given in a court of law and comes with the same penalties of perjury.

• Always reply honestly and as accurately as possible

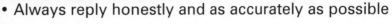

Tales of the Transcript

Court Reporter: Do you solemnly swear that the testimony you are about to give will be the truth, the whole truth, and nothing but the truth, so help you God?

Witness: I'll try

More Humor in the Court, p. 30.

• **The court reporter will transcribe every spoken word.** Therefore, head shakes or nods cannot be recorded by the court reporter. Also, a court reporter can only transcribe what is being said by one person at a time.

• **If you do not understand a question, say so.** If you do answer my question, I will assume you understood and answered the question asked.

- **Please do not guess in response to my questions**. However, I am entitled to your best estimate. Do you understand the difference between a guess and an estimate?
- **Your testimony will be transcribed into a booklet.** You will have the opportunity to review your testimony and make any changes you deem appropriate. You will then sign your deposition transcript under penalty of perjury. However, if you make any substantive changes to your testimony, either I or the other counsel may comment on your changes at trial and it may adversely affect your credibility.
- I therefore request you **give me your best testimony today.** Is there any reason you cannot go forward with providing your best testimony today?
- **Are you under the influence of any drugs, alcohol or medications that may affect your ability to respond to my questions?**

● ● ● ● ● ● ● ● ●

Tales of the Transcript

Listen carefully to every word in the question and make certain that you understand it before you reply.

Q: Are you currently taking any medications that impact your ability to remember?

A: Can you repeat the question?

- **Do you have any questions regarding the deposition before we start?***

*Tyson, *Ibid.*

Opposing counsel usually carefully plans the timing of the most important questions. Beware that they may be saved for the end of the deposition or posed at a time when you are bored, angry, tired, or ready for a lunch break.* All questions are important and are potentially damaging if not answered properly.

● ● ● ● ● ● ● ●

Tales of the Transcript

Some lawyers do not ask the most artful questions at times. For example:

Q: Now doctor, isn't it true that when a person dies in his sleep, he doesn't know about it until the next morning?

• • • • • • •

Q: You say the stairs went down to the basement?

A: Yes.

Q: And these stairs, did they go up also?

AN ADMISSION

Beware that anything you say can be treated as an admission that might be used against you in trial or to support a Summary Judgment Motion before trial. **For this reason, you have to listen carefully to each word of each question. If you understand the question, pause and think about it carefully, phrase your reply in your mind, and then slowly and clearly reply as concisely as possible.**

● ● ● ● ● ● ● ●

Tales of the Transcript

Always pause before you reply to make certain you understand the question and to give your lawyer an opportunity to object to the question.

In a lawsuit involving a hotel, a witness was asked:

Q: Have you ever stayed at the Residence Inn?

A: Yes, for my honeymoon ten years ago.

Q: Was it a pleasant experience?

A: Well, hello????

Objection – please rephrase the question.

Courtesy of Bud Furr, Esq.

When you are asked a question, do not look at your lawyer or another friendly party that may be in attendance as to how to reply. It is improper for them to signal or coach you in any way. They cannot answer for you – just do the best you can. If you are well prepared that will not be a problem.

● ● ● ● ● ● ● ●

Tales of the Transcript

Hopefully the lawyer that asked the question below immediately said "strike that" last question after realizing what he asked.

Q: So the date of conception of the baby was August 8th?

A: Yes.

Q: And what were you doing at that time?

Disorder in the Court, p. 64

ADMIT YOU CONSULTED YOUR LAWYER

You will likely be asked "With whom did you discuss your deposition?" or "Did your lawyer tell you what to say?" You should say that you talked with your lawyer and he told you to answer truthfully. Do not reveal what you discussed with your lawyer, as those conversations are privileged and you do not have to disclose them. **Your lawyer should promptly object to any such inquiries.**

Remember you have nothing to hide, there is no need to respond defensively; all lawyers as a rule meet with the deponent prior to their depositions.

● ● ● ● ● ● ● ●

Tales of the Transcript

Some actual questions from depositions that obviously should not have been asked.

Q: Was it you or your younger brother who was killed in the war?

• • • •

Q: How far apart were the vehicles at the time of the collision?

• • • •

Q: You were there until the time you left, is that true?

• • • •

Q: How many times have you committed suicide?

• • • •

Q: Did he kill you?

Most, if not all attorneys will advise you to dress conservatively for your deposition. You should dress as though your deposition will be videotaped. Select business dress over casual, dark colors over bright ones, solids over prints and no flashy jewelry. Make-up use should be toned-down and discrete. In other words, do not dress in a manner that draws attention to your clothing.

Remember that the opposition attorney and your lawyer will each form an opinion of the type of impression you will make at trial based on your appearance and demeanor at your deposition.

● ● ● ● ● ● ● ●

Tales of the Transcript

As part of your deposition preparation, you must become familiar with some of the basic terminology you may encounter.

Q: Is your appearance this morning pursuant to a deposition notice which I sent to your attorney?

A: No, this is how I dress when I go to work.

More Humor in the Court, p. 40

POSTURE AT A DEPOSITION

Your attitude toward the litigation can be reflected in your posture. Keep your feet on the floor, sit erect, leaning slightly forward. Do not recline or lean back in your chair. Try not to indicate anxiety by wiggling your feet or legs, rocking back and forth, or drumming your fingers, tapping your pen, etc.

● ● ● ● ● ● ● ●

Tales of the Transcript

In *SEC v. Pinn Fund* (S.D. Cal.), I was prosecuting the former CEO of a subprime mortgage lender and his porn star girlfriend. The claim against the girlfriend was that she had improperly received the fruits of the fraud in the form of jewelry, a $5 million home in Laguna Niguel, etc. Her primary defense was that she had "given value" for these things and was thus entitled to them. We noticed her videotaped deposition, and we figured she'd show up conservatively dressed. She showed up in a tight mini-skirt and low cut blouse with fur trim reminiscent of a boa. In her deposition, she claimed that the "value" given had nothing to do with what one might think in light of her attire. The trial was very short. Lesson: dress appropriately, especially if you're going to be filmed.

Courtesy of Nick Morgan, Esq.

DEMEANOR AT YOUR DEPOSITION

During your deposition, you should conduct yourself as if you were in a courtroom, in front of a judge or jury. In fact, you should consider yourself under observation from the time you enter the building until you exit it.

● ● ● ● ● ● ● ● ●

Tales of the Transcript

Even one of the world's most respected business executives can come across at his deposition poorly if he is not properly prepared as to how he will be perceived by his replies and actions/mannerisms (if videotaped).

This Version of Bill Gates Has a Memory Problem

His Videotaped testimony shows a chief exec who often can't recall key E-mail exchanges.

Maybe there are two Bill Gates. Gates I is the confident and dynamic entrepreneur who strides before the public at Microsoft-boosting events. Gates II is the chief executive slouching behind a table on a videotaped deposition, rocking as he reads documents, and often telling government prosecutors that he can't recall having written E-mails to Microsoft execs on key company issues. And there was some hair-splitting parsing of words: "Depends on what you mean by 'compete,'" Gates said at one point, in an exchange that seemed eerily similar to the other Bill's exchange on the word, "is."

Business Week On-Line, November 2, 1998.

DO NOT TALK TO THE OPPONENT

It is all right to greet briefly the other side but do not enter into discussions or pleasantries with the other side or their counsel. They will be attempting to get information from you that they can use against you any way they can. Do not before, during, or after your deposition talk to your opponent or their lawyer. They are your legal enemies. If they cause you to drop your guard, you may reveal some information damaging to your case. Do not lose sight of the fact that the other side is your enemy and are there to defeat you and your side.

Never discuss your deposition with your opponent. If you do, you may inadvertently provide the other side with additional evidence to use against you.

Do not be friendly to the other side; be polite. The other side will appear to be your friend and try to help you, but they only really want to score points for their side. So do not be charmed into a false sense of security by an opposing counsel or party. The opposing lawyer is not your friend, no matter how friendly or accommodating he is. Be courteous, but be vigilant.

WARNING

LEGAL ENEMIES

OPPOSING OPPONENT
COUNSEL

DO NOT MEMORIZE YOUR ANSWERS

Be prepared for the types of questions that might be asked but do not memorize your answers. Questions will never be posed exactly as you practiced and expect, and your set answers may not be totally appropriate and you may get easily confused. In any event, rehearsed answers and testimony usually sound false and too smooth. Then, when you are asked a question that you did not expect or anticipate, and you stumble with your reply, it may seem as though you are being evasive or lying.

Your deposition is your opportunity to show the other side the strengths of your case. So make certain you refresh your memory about the key facts in the case so that you can respond confidently and accurately when questioned. Remember that you are playing defense, not trying to win the case, but you must be fully prepared to respond appropriately and intelligently.

● ● ● ● ● ● ● ●

Tales of the Transcript

Your replies should be consistent with one another; if not, the accuracy of all of your answers may be challenged.

Q: How old is your son, the one living with you?

A: Thirty-eight or thirty-five, I can't remember which.

Q: How long has he lived with you?

A: Forty-five years.

LISTEN CAREFULLY TO THE FULL QUESTION

Do not interrupt the questioner; do not try to anticipate the rest of the question. Listen to the entire question, pause and think it over to determine if you understand it; then, if so, proceed with your reply.

● ● ● ● ● ● ●

Tales of the Transcript

Make certain you understand every question completely before you attempt a reply.

Q: What gear were you in at the moment of the impact?

A: Gucci sweats and Reeboks.

Be sure to maintain eye contact with the lawyer questioning you. Looking away is often taken by some to indicate feelings of guilt or inferiority, and rapid eye movement is generally taken by body language experts to indicate desperate thought.*

● ● ● ● ● ● ●

Tales of the Transcript

Q: How was your first marriage terminated?

A: By death.

Q: And by whose death was it terminated?

*www.jesbeard.com

DO NOT BE AFRAID

There is no one who is going to hurt you and there is no need to show fear or anxiety or to be afraid to answer a question truthfully.

● ● ● ● ● ● ●

Tales of the Transcript

Remember in a deposition there is no time clock so take the time you require to formulate and provide your reply. Of course, if you are being videotaped you have to reply promptly.

Q: What is your brother-in-law's name?

A: Borofkin.

Q: What's his first name.

A: I can't remember.

Q: He's been your brother-in-law for years, and you can't remember his first name?

A: No, I tell you I'm too excited. (Rising from the witness chair and pointing to Mr. Borofkin) Nathan, for God's sake, tell them your first name!

PAUSE BEFORE YOU ANSWER

Pause before you reply to any question. This gives you an opportunity to think over the question fully. There is no time clock or a jury present so your speed of reply is not important (unless you are being videotaped) and should not generally be reflected in the written transcript. Additionally, when you pause, it provides your attorney an opportunity to pose an objection to the question if one is warranted. If you answer before your lawyer objects, you might inadvertently reveal information that could harm your case. This does not mean that you should try to delay the deposition by taking excessive time to answer a question, but simply that you should make sure you give yourself time to fully understand it, and to allow your attorney to object to it, before answering.

Tales of the Transcript

Do not be afraid to make your questioner work for his answers; just do not overdo it.

Q: On the evening of the incident what time did you serve dinner?

A: When the oven buzzer went off.

BE AUDIBLE

A court reporter can only hear and record what comes out of your mouth. Therefore, do not nod your head yes or no, shrug, or reply with "uh-huh," "yup," etc. Remember that every question and every answer will be recorded by the court reporter. Sometimes the reporter may not be able to distinguish an "uh-huh" (yes) from ""uh-uh" (no) and the wrong reply will be recorded. To avoid this problem, yes or no replies should be clearly stated as "yes, Sir" or "no, Sir." Speak loudly enough so every person in the deposition room can hear you clearly, especially the court reporter. Otherwise, the court reporter will continuously interrupt you for you to repeat your response. Do not chew gum. Keep your fingers and hands away from your mouth.

●　　●　　●　　●　　●　　●　　●

Tales of the Transcript

If your replies are not consistent, the inconsistent replies will really stand out.

Q: Did you ever stay all night with this man in New York?

A: I refuse to answer that question.

Q: Did you ever stay all night with this man in Chicago?

A: I refuse to answer that question.

Q: Did you ever stay all night with this man in Miami?

A: No.

Be humble, polite and respectful. A humble witness usually comes across as being more credible.

● ● ● ● ● ● ●

Tales of the Transcript

Q: Doctor, would you be surprised if you saw the defendant talking to himself?

A: Not in the least.

Q: Why is that?

A: He doesn't have any friends.

Disorderly Conduct, pp 122-103.

TELL THE TRUTH

You are sworn by the court reporter to tell the truth and you should answer every question truthfully. In this manner, you will, hopefully, not be caught in inconsistencies, will not have to worry about prior replies, and will be better able to relax and respond. If you tell the truth, you will not have to stop and think whether a truthful answer will help or hurt your case. When you tell the truth accurately, no one can confuse you. A lie may lose the case. You must tell the truth, which is more than merely not telling an intentional lie.

Most lawyers will advise that if the truth hurts, so be it. However, good lawyers will make strong and reasoned efforts to explain why the truth should not be as damaging as the opponent may try to suggest. But it is not possible to explain a lie away.

Also, testifying falsely in a deposition constitutes perjury, and is a crime. You do irreparable damage to your employer or yourself if you are caught lying and you may subject yourself to possible civil or criminal penalties. Do not lie. Tell the truth.

No one can be expected to recall every detail surrounding a pending case. If you do not know the answer to a question, reply that you do not know. If you do not remember, simply say you do not recall or you do not remember. **If you go ahead and speculate or make improper assumptions, it may be used against you later.**

If you reply that "you do not know" at your deposition, it is very difficult at trial to testify and know something you did not know years or even months earlier. If you do not know the answer to a question, even if you think that you will appear evasive or stupid stating you do not know, you should still say you do not know, as a guess or estimate is always wrong. You should, however, distinguish between things you do not know, and never knew, and things you do not remember. If you believe you once knew something, you should say you do not remember, not that you do not know. That way, you will have the ability to refresh your recollection by looking at documents, or talking to other people, before trial, which may allow you to testify at trial to something you could not remember during your deposition without appearing to contradict an answer that said you "did not know" the relevant fact.

Never try to make up an answer, even if you have a good guess as to what the answer is or is likely to be. If you are asked to speculate and your lawyer permits you to do so, make it clear in your answer that you are merely speculating.

● ● ● ● ● ● ●

Tales of the Transcript

Make certain you understand the questions you are being asked; otherwise, you may provide a damaging admission or a foolish reply.

Q: Sir, what is your IQ?

A: Well, I can see pretty well, I think.

BE BRIEF AND CONCISE

All of your replies should be as short and concise as possible. It is not your role to tell the opposing side everything you know. Remember, you can do very little in your deposition to help your case, but you can do much to harm it. You cannot win your case in your deposition, but you can lose it if you are not careful.

Your job, when providing your deposition is to remember to play defense and to avoid volunteering information to the other side. When you add more to your answers, you merely provide the examining attorney with more ammunition to use against you and the longer your deposition will last. Remember as a general rule the four best answers you can provide (unless you are asked a leading question) are:

- "Yes."

- "No."

- "I do not know."

- "I do not recall."

If you are asked a leading question or a series of leading questions, do not reply with these four responses unless you must do so to answer truthfully. If you do it will only allow the opposing lawyer to put words in your mouth. You should listen very carefully to all leading questions, because lawyers will often load such questions up with things that you might not believe are true. Thus, if there is an inaccurate assumption or premise in a leading question, you should feel free to challenge or correct it before responding.

● ● ● ● ● ● ●

Tales of the Transcript

A good example of brief and concise replies took place in this case:

Q. And you had an affair with the boss?

A. Yes.

Q. When did this affair begin?

A. Late one night in the office.

Q. And how long did this affair last?

A. About 15 minutes.

Courtesy of Joseph Collins, Esq.

The other side will use your deposition to search for as much information as possible. Do not help them by volunteering information. It will only open further areas of inquiry, further prolong your deposition, and reveal facts, witnesses and documents that the opposing party may not otherwise know. Do not bring up matters you are not asked about. Beware that most experienced lawyers sense deponents who wish to volunteer information. These lawyers will merely sit there quietly or nod their heads in the direction of the deponent so that the deponent feels obligated to volunteer information and continues to reply. Do not fall into this trap.

Tales of the Transcript

A number of years ago, I defended the deposition of a VP-level witness who I prepared for the deposition by, among other things, reminding him of the cardinal rules for testifying in a deposition: listening to the question, thinking about the answer and then answering the question without volunteering information beyond the parameters of the question. My witness learned those rules so well, most of his answers started with "I know I am not supposed to volunteer anything, but…" Instead of 2 or 3 hours, his deposition lasted nearly two days of 6 hour sessions.

Courtesy of Ronald Yin, Esq.

Tales of the Transcript

A drug company's head of drug safety and labeling was being prepared for a deposition in a products case where the key issue was the adequacy of the label. From previous depositions, the lawyer preparing him knew the witness was prone to go far afield when answering questions. Thus, the lawyer really tried to impress on the witness the need to listen to each question, answer only the specific question as phrased, not to volunteer information and so forth. The obvious question was asked at the deposition: "Do you think the drug label was adequate?" After some extended thought, the witness said "No." This being inconsistent with his prior views, his lawyer asked him on a break why on earth he had answered that way. His answer: "Because the label was more than adequate but you told me not to volunteer information."

Courtesy of Ronald Yin, Esq.

DO NOT OVER ANSWER

Do not over answer. For example, the ideal answer to "Do you have the time?" would be, "Yes." You do not need to expand by responding "Yes, it is 2 pm" or "to tell him how to build a watch." Each word you use will be scrutinized. Too much information gives the other side time to ask additional questions and open new areas of inquiry, identify more people to depose. The longer your answers, the longer the deposition. Do not over answer or feel compelled to explain or justify your reply.*

●　　●　　●　　●　　●　　●　　●

Tales of the Transcript

It is not your job to make it easier for the opposing lawyer. An example of concise, accurate replies follows:

Q. Where do you live?

A. Terre Haute, Indiana.

Q. Have you lived in Terre Haute your entire life?

A. Not yet.

Courtesy of Joseph Collins, Esq.

DO NOT FILL IN PERIODS OF SILENCE

Once you have completed your answer, shut your mouth and stay silent. Counsel will frequently remain silent after your reply to see if you will continue and volunteer some useful information. People frequently are uncomfortable with silence and feel compelled to fill the void. Do not be tempted to do so, even if the questioner pauses for a minute or longer. Instead of answering the question as briefly as possible and stopping, the talkative witness goes on and on, adding all sorts of colorful details and personal observations or opinions. Opposing counsel loves this because it often provides new and interesting details that can open up new areas of inquiry, new people to depose, new documents to review or can cause damage in court before a jury.*

*Wahl, *Op. cit.*

IF YOU ARE INTERRUPTED

If you are interrupted during your reply and desire to complete your reply, merely tell the opposing attorney that you did not complete your answer and wish to do so.

● ● ● ● ● ● ●

Tales of the Transcript

Try not to laugh at opposing counsel if he asks a foolish question; it serves no useful purpose to get him angry with you.

Q: Can you describe the individual?

A: The person was about medium height and had a beard.

Q: Was this a male or a female?

If you are not certain of the reply to a question or do not know the answer, it is best to say you do not know or that you do not recall.

● ● ● ● ● ● ●

Tales of the Transcript

It is important to be accurate, but not to the point of stupidity:

In an age discrimination claim, the plaintiff was allegedly terminated for engaging in threatening behavior. In his deposition, he was asked

Q: "Who is Mr. B?"

A: "My Beretta gun."

Q: "Isn't it true that on June 5th, you got in an argument with a co-worker and told him he better be careful because Mr. B had taken a ride with you in your car that day and could solve the dispute?" After a lengthy pause and apparent deep thinking, the witness said –

A: "It didn't happen on June 5th."

Courtesy of Charles Vinicombe, Esq.

DO NOT TRY TO JUSTIFY OR EXPLAIN YOUR REPLY

Once you have finished your answer, keep quiet. Do not feel compelled to explain or justify your reply, even if your reply is followed by a period of silence by the examining attorney. You are at the deposition to provide facts known to you and you are not obligated nor required to attempt to justify those facts or apologize. If you do attempt to do so, it will undermine the accuracy of your testimony, prolong your deposition and result in errors.

Once you respond, stop talking. There is no need to elaborate or volunteer as to how or why you arrived at your conclusion.

● ● ● ● ● ● ●

Tales of the Transcript

Weigh your replies carefully because how you respond can clearly impact your credibility.

When the Department of Justice deposed Bill Gates, chairman of Microsoft, Inc. in an antitrust case, Mr. Gates came across as being "evasive and non-responsive" when asked to verify a quote attributed to him in a published article. He said he would have to review the transcript of the interview to see its full content before commenting.

DO NOT TRY TO BE A HELPFUL WITNESS

Like talkative witnesses, helpful witnesses provide more information than is necessary. They feel compelled to fill in the gaps, to explain, to justify. They sometimes try to "help" themselves or their company by saying what they assume will be the "right" answer, even if they do not have personal knowledge of the truth. Opposing counsel love helpful witnesses, because they often help the other side find contradictions between testimony and fact.*

● ● ● ● ● ● ●

Tales of the Transcript

Q: What is your name?

A: [states name]

Q: And what is your marital status?

A: Fair.

*Wahl, *Op. cit.*

AVOID ABSOLUTES

Try to avoid when testifying saying "always," "never," etc. It sets you up to be contradicted by strong cross-examination at trial. Instead of responding "no," "never," it is better to reply "not that I can recall."

Beware of questions that use words such as "never" or "always" as one single exception can make you look like a liar.

If you do not understand a question, tell the lawyer you do not understand or ask him to rephrase it. Do not answer a question you do not understand and never ask opposing counsel "do you mean?" Do not do his job for him and do not make his job easier for him.

● ● ● ● ● ● ●

Tales of the Transcript

This amusing exchange took place in a divorce case.

Q: What was the first thing your husband said to you when he woke that morning?

A: He said, "Where am I, Cathy?"

Q: And why did that upset you?

A: My name is Susan.

THERE IS NO "OFF THE RECORD"

In any deposition, there is no such thing as "off the record." If you talk to any one in the room, where you are being deposed – be prepared to be questioned about it. This holds true for any notes or records you make during your deposition or bring with you to the deposition. (When the lawyers agree to go "off the record" it merely means that the stenographer will not record what is said; it does *not* mean that the opposing lawyer will not listen to and question you about things you say "off the record").

Your testimony will be under oath. You will be sworn to tell the truth by the court reporter. The court reporter will record every comment made during the deposition, unless the parties agree to a recess, break or go "off the record." Beware, however, that unless all parties agree, you may not "go off the record."

Tales of the Transcript

Again, make certain you understand the question before you answer.

Q: Did you blow your horn or anything?

A: After the accident?

Q: Before the accident.

A: Sure, I played for ten years. I even went to school for it.

YOU WILL NOT PITCH A SHUTOUT

Tales of the Transcript

You may not win your case in your deposition, but you can certainly lose it. A male Teamster truck driver suing for sexual harassment based on the off-color remarks of his petite female dispatcher responded as follows:

Q: Well, didn't you use profanity in the workplace yourself?

A: Oh sure. We all swore like truck drivers, because that's what we were.

No matter how well-prepared you are, expect the other side to score some points during your testimony. Be as prepared as possible to reduce the damage that may occur. If you make a mistake, put it aside and move along without calling attention to it.

If at any time during your deposition you discover that you have provided a wrong reply or have misspoken, try to correct your reply once you recognize your mistake by telling the opposing lawyer or your lawyer at the first possible opportunity. Otherwise, you run the risk of forgetting and many other questions and replies can be built on mistaken information that could damage your case or, at a minimum, extend your deposition if the error is not corrected promptly.

IF YOU DO NOT REMEMBER

If, in fact, you do not recall something, never be fearful of saying you do not recall. Do not say "that is all I know." Later you may recall something else, so it is better to say "that is all I recall at this time." If you are testifying about injuries to you, do not say "those are all my injuries." You can describe your injuries and how your activities are affected, but always add "there may be more, but that is all I can recall at this moment."

If you reply "I do not remember" too often it could come back to hurt you as it could be used to help get your case dismissed or could damage your credibility at trial if you then know the answers.

● ● ● ● ● ● ●

Tales of the Transcript

While it might be normal for witnesses not to remember events that are routine, it might seem odd if they do not remember events that are remarkable.

One witness, being pressed about why he did not have a good memory of a given event, pointed out to the lawyer: "I don't recall what I had for dinner a week ago, but if I had buffalo I would remember."

If during your deposition you realize you now remember something or that you need to correct a prior reply, you should interrupt the questioner and advise that you now remember something or you can now better provide a more accurate or complete reply to an earlier question. It is not unusual for your memory to be refreshed during the course of your deposition as questions are asked and documents reviewed. Therefore, it is perfectly acceptable for you to recall items as your deposition proceeds as no one can be expected to clearly, accurately and completely recall past events.

● ● ● ● ● ● ●

Tales of the Transcript

In a personal injury deposition of a plaintiff who conveniently lacked recollection of critical issues:

Q: Has any healthcare provider ever advised you that you suffer from any memory defect?
A: I don't recall.

Courtesy of Paul Dougherty, Esq.

DO NOT TALK TO OTHERS

Do not talk to others about the litigation or your deposition. Talking results in evidence that you may not intend or want to create. Do not ask other witnesses about their depositions, and do not answer questions about yours. You may be asked during the deposition whether you have talked with anyone else about the deposition and if you did, anything that you said or someone else said become subject to discovery. The only person you should talk to about your deposition is your attorney. If, in special circumstances, your attorney wants you to discuss matters with other people, he will advise you on what to do.

IF YOU ARE ASKED ABOUT
YOUR INTERROGATORY RESPONSES

If you responded to written questions under oath (Interrogatories) and the opposing attorney wants you to elaborate on your written answer or explain it to him, tell the attorney that you prepared those responses with your counsel's help and therefore, you cannot answer the question at the deposition without his assistance.* Note, however, that you may properly impose this limitation on your answers only insofar as the deposition questions would reveal privileged communications; you cannot use this objection to conceal the underlying facts that support your interrogatory answers.

● ● ● ● ● ● ●

Tales of the Transcript

If you realize you made a mistake in your testimony, at the first available opportunity point out your error and correct it.

Q: So, you are unconscious, and they pulled you from the pool. What happened then?

A: Mr. Stewart gave me artificial insemination – you know, mouth-to-mouth.

*Frank D. Granato, "Are Your Prepared for Your Deposition?" expertlaw.com, 2004

DO NOT ANSWER A QUESTION THAT
ASKS YOU TO STATE ALL THE FACTS THAT
SUPPORT YOUR CONTENTION OR DEFENSE

If the attorney asks you to state the facts that support your defense, your response is simply I do not know.* Do not answer a question that asks you to state all the facts that support your contention or defense, you do not have to know that reply, that is your lawyer's job, not yours. Your lawyer should interpose an objection to make that clear during your deposition if this question is asked, but you should be prepared to respond to it in case he does not.

*Granato, *Ibid.*

DO NOT TRY TO OUTWIT THE OPPOSING LAWYER

Do not try to anticipate where the lawyer's line of questioning is going and do not try to outwit him. Your job is to concentrate on each and every question as it is asked and to reply as accurately and concisely as possible.

● ● ● ● ● ● ●

Tales of the Transcript

Make sure you formulate your reply as fully in your mind, as possible, before you answer.

Q: And what did you see when [the accused] pulled down his pants?
A: It looked like a penis, only smaller.

More Humor in the Court, p. 54

DO NOT TRY TO BE A CLEVER WITNESS

Do not be a witness who thinks he is smarter than the opposing lawyer or can out smart him or who is afraid to ask for clarification. If you are, you may give a reply without fully understanding the question or may foolishly try to be intentionally evasive or non-responsive. The clever witness, when faced with a choice between admitting ignorance or making up a response, tends to go ahead and answer, with predictably bad results. Clever witnesses are generally easy for the other side to trip up later in court.*

*Wahl, *Op. cit.*

DO NOT GET ANGRY

Depositions are like verbal fisticuffs, and occasionally there is actual physical confrontation. Once when I was in a deposition with my firm in New York, an attorney from the other side reached over the table and physically grabbed papers because I did not give them to him. Another time in New York when I was a young associate, I was verbally attacked mercilessly by a senior partner in one of the big firms because he did not like how I was besting the associate from his firm who was taking the deposition. On a third occasion, here in California, an attorney taking the deposition lost his temper, pounded his fist on the table and lunged across the table at me before he calmed down.

Courtesy of Steven Berger, Esq.

Even if you get upset or angry during your deposition, do not let it show. Some lawyers will intentionally try to incite you or trick you into saying or doing something you will regret. Stay as calm as possible. Keep an even tone of voice and be consistent and steady in your reply to each question. Do not demonstrate hostility – it could hurt your case. If you remain calm under provocation, it will help your case.

Therefore, regardless of the question, do not get mad and do not argue with the opposing counsel. Any argument is for your lawyer to handle, not you. If your lawyer does get involved in an argument with the other attorney (and this does happen from time to time, especially in cases that last a long time), stay out of the argument. Leave it to your attorney.

If you get angry you may lose your cool and answer without thinking and this could seriously damage your case. An angry witness is never an effective one.

DO NOT BE ANXIOUS TO LEAVE

If the opposing attorney views you as relaxed, comfortable
and not in a hurry to leave, he is likely to make it a short
deposition. But, if he notices that you are agitated or uncomfortable, and that you cannot wait for a break to occur, he will
prolong the deposition and even become more aggressive in
his approach.* Therefore, do not be anxious to leave.

Tales of the Transcript

There was a time when I took a red eye
to Chicago in the freezing cold and was
very late because of the ice. I started
questioning a very big name chairperson
at the University of Chicago, the father of
paramedicine about a death case involving paramedics using an adult bag and
mask on a one year old and blowing him
up like a balloon. I had been reading a
Bender treatise on the *Art of Cross Examination of Medical Experts*. I was so tired
when I started, I couldn't find my papers.
I fumbled for a good 20 minutes not asking a single good question whereupon
my learned opponent said "God damn
it John, you dragged us to Chicago and

*Granato, *Op. cit.*

BEWARE OF THE OPPOSING LAWYER PLAYING DUMB

As a strategy, the opposing counsel wants you to think that he does not know or understand the particular subject matter of your deposition or the case. This is to try to draw you out so you give more detailed and elaborate replies to educate him. This is not likely the case. Lawyers are required to bone-up on the subject matter of the litigation and good lawyers become as knowledgeable in the facts and subject matter of the litigation as expert witnesses in the case and the parties themselves.

You should assume that the deposing attorney either already knows the correct answer to the question, or he will know the proper reply prior to trial. So if you are asked a question requiring a detailed reply, be sure to note that "this is all I recall at the moment."

● ● ● ● ● ● ●

have not asked a single decent question." Inspired, I found my stride:

Q: Now Doctor, with your skills and abilities, certainly you could have brought Bobby into the hospital alive, right?

A: Well, of course I could have kept him alive.

Q: Well, Doctor, that would also be true of any reasonably skilled paramedic who had been properly trained by someone familiar with the principles in your textbook on paramedicine which is in use intergalactically, right?

A: Certainly.

I believe I sunk that set of hooks four more times, leaving my sputtering opponent trying to recant his testimony after some hallway conversations (before the rules changed).

Which led me to the question about those exchanges and to sink the hook so badly that case settled within a week.

Lesson: never irritate your opponent unduly or unnecessarily. He might wake up.

Courtesy: John Robert Holland, Esq.

AVOID INDEFINITE PRONOUNS

Make certain everyone can follow your pronoun use; he, she, they, it, them, their. Refer to people by their names to allow everyone to keep track of exactly whom you are discussing.*

● ● ● ● ● ● ●

Tales of the Transcript

This is a good example of an accurate and polite reply that clearly points out that the question was improperly phrased The attorney for the deponent should have objected as to the form of the question.

Q: Doctor, as a result of your examination of the plaintiff, is the young lady pregnant?

A: The young lady is pregnant – but not as a result of my examination.

DESCRIPTIVE WORDS AND PHRASES

Beware of descriptive words and phrases in questions like:

- Often

- Slow

- Sometimes

- Many

- Constantly

- Small number, etc.

These words depend on their context and mean different things to different people. Therefore, ask the lawyer to rephrase the question or to be more specific.

● ● ● ● ● ● ●

Tales of the Transcript

Q: Any suggestions as to what prevented this from being a murder trial instead of an attempted murder trial?

A: The victim lived.

QUESTIONS ASKED IN THE NEGATIVE

Some lawyers will pose questions in the negative to give the impression that they have already verified the data they are requesting. For example, "Didn't you mention to the plaintiff she was not promoted because she was a female?" Beware of this technique and reply appropriately. If a question has a double negative, do not answer it. Ask the lawyer to restate the question without using a double negative.

● ● ● ● ● ● ●

Tales of the Transcript

In a civil right case, the Sheriff was asked:

Q: Did you make a conscious decision as the Sheriff of Gilpin County not to investigate the hanging of Roy Smith, a black man, who was reported having been hung upside down from a beam in his house?

A: Well I guess it was not unconscious.

Courtesy of John Robert Holland, Esq.

DO NOT SHOW INDICATIONS OF FATIGUE, BOREDOM, ETC.

Control your expressions, even if you are bored out of your mind, totally frustrated, or tired. The other side will look for such opportunities to catch you off-guard with a question that could result in a potentially damaging remark. If you are tired and lose focus, do not hesitate to request a short break.*

Mental fatigue and loss of concentration starts to occur after about 40 minutes of answering questions. Do not be afraid to ask to take a break. Do this as often as necessary. You do yourself a disservice by trying to get the deposition over with and risk giving sloppy answers that will come back to haunt you at trial.

Remember, as stated earlier, do not to let your guard down right before lunch break and at the very end of your deposition.

*www.rmf.harvard.edu/crico

DO NOT MAKE JOKES

Do not make jokes as the written record when read almost never comes across as being funny and more importantly, if you do it, it will give opposing counsel an opportunity to ask "so you think this is funny?" Always remember litigation is serious business. Wisecracks and jokes upon reading the transcript frequently come across as being cold and inappropriate.

● ● ● ● ● ● ●

Tales of the Transcript

Even though at times during your deposition you may be tempted to make a joke or or respond harshly, resist the urge to do so.

Q: When was the last time you saw the deceased?

A: At his funeral.

Q: Did he make any comments to you at that time?

Tales of the Transcript

An experienced witness that is known to the lawyers and judge (like a medical examiner) might get away with the following replies, but you should not attempt it.

Q: Doctor, before you performed the autopsy, did you check for a pulse?

A: No.

Q: Did you check for blood pressure?

A: No.

Q: Did you check for breathing?

A: No.

Q: So, then it is possible that the patient was alive when you began the autopsy?

A: No.

Q: How can you be so sure, Doctor?

A: Because his brain was sitting on my desk in a jar.

Q: But could the patient have still been alive nevertheless?

A: Yes, it is possible that he could have been alive and practicing law somewhere.

DO NOT MAKE INSENSITIVE COMMENTS

Do not express offensive comments about race, gender, religion, national origins, etc. If you do, you risk offending someone and it could be used against you at trial.

● ● ● ● ● ● ●

Tales of the Transcript

Again, resist the urge to respond with a wisecrack when you are asked a ridiculous question.

Q: Were you alone in the car?

A: Yes.

Q: Were you driving?

More Humor in the Court, p. 27

Do not be sarcastic; sarcastic comments are not well received when reduced to a transcript. You could come across as arrogant, rude, and/or mean-spirited.

● ● ● ● ● ● ●

Tales of the Transcript

Although the following exchange is funny, if read to a jury during a trial you could come across as being arrogant or a wise-aleck. It is best not to make jokes.

Q: Do you recall the time that you examined the body?

A: The autopsy started around 8:30 p.m.

Q: And Mr. Dennington was dead at the time?

A: No, he was sitting on the table wondering why I was doing an autopsy.

DO NOT CALL SOMEONE A LIAR

Remember that if you call someone a liar, it may be difficult to get the jury to believe that person or anything he has to say that might help your case. Unless you honestly believe a person is a liar, it is better for you to not call him a liar, better to say "he is mistaken on that point."*

•　•　•　•　•　•　•

Tales of the Transcript

Q: Mrs. Smith, do you believe you are emotionally unstable?

A: I used to be.

Q: How many times have you committed suicide?

A: Four times.

More Humor in the Court, p. 17

LOOK OUT FOR COMPOUND QUESTIONS

Lawyers at times ask more than one question at a time. Go slowly and state you can only respond to one question at a time. Do not reply to a compound question. Your lawyer should object to compound questions as to its form. If not, you should ask that they be broken into separate questions. For example, if asked "Isn't it true that you know the defendent and you attended the same college and dated the same girl?" merely request the lawyer to please ask only one question at a time.

LOOK OUT FOR CERTAIN INTRODUCTORY PHRASES

Be especially alert when counsel begins a question by using any of the following introductory phrases:

- "You testified that…"

- "If I could summarize your answer, you said…"

- "Do you agree in principle that…"

- "Is it fair to say that…"

Leading questions such as these are frequently followed by statements that may be partial truths or facts that you do not know to be true. Do not let the deposing counsel place you in a position of adopting partial truths or unknown facts. Do not reply "yes" or "no" to these questions. These are exceptions to the rule to be brief and concise. If you are asked a leading question or a series of leading questions, take time to explain what is wrong with the question as framed and be certain you point out what is wrong or what you disagree with concerning the questions and reply appropriately.

● ● ● ● ● ● ●

Tales of the Transcript

If it is not a leading question, there is no need to explain your answer – just reply and stay quiet.

Q: Did you kill the victim?

A: No, I did not.

Q: Do you know what the penalties are for perjury?

A: Yes, I do. And they're a hell of a lot better than the penalty for murder.

WATCH OUT FOR SUMMARIES OF YOUR TESTIMONY

Be especially cautious if the opposing lawyer asks you a question that summarizes your prior testimony. Be absolutely certain it is accurate so he is not putting words into your mouth. Do not endorse or agree to any summary unless every aspect of it is correct.

Watch out for questions that paraphrase your answers. Often the attorney will modify your reply and use it in a manner you did not mean by putting it in new words. If the attorney does that and asks if that is what you meant, responding "yes" could damage your case. If the lawyer asks if his paraphrasing is accurate, you should say you wish to stand by your answer the way you phrased it.

● ● ● ● ● ● ●

Tales of the Transcript

The following exchange took place in a deposition of a bitterly contested divorce suit:

Q: Isn't it a fact that you have been running around with another woman?

A: Yes, it is, but you can't prove it!

IS THAT ALL?

Beware of questions that ask "is that all?" The opposing law-yer is trying to lock your testimony in. You should respond "to the best of my knowledge at this time." **Leave the door open in the event you recall more information during your deposition or at trial.**

● ● ● ● ● ● ●

Tales of the Transcript

If possible, it is best (unless asked a lead-ing question) to reply "yes," "no," "I do not know" or "I do not recall."

Q: And y'all had a very intimate relation-ship, didn't you Mrs. A?

A: We had sex two times. It wasn't very intimate.

Disorder in the Court, page 222.

Be careful if the phrases "Is that right?" or "Is that correct?" are used at the end of a question. It usually calls for a "yes" or "no" response and it may not be clear what you are saying yes or no to. For example, "you did not tell your boss you had a disability, is that right?" If you reply "no" it could be the response to two different parts of the question. So specify in your answer what you are replying to and keep the record clear. "Yes, I did not advise my boss."

● ● ● ● ● ● ●

Tales of the Transcript

During a divorce proceeding, the following occurred.

Q: Isn't it true that on the night of June 11, in a prune orchard at such and such a location, you had relations with Mr. Blank on the back of his motorcycle? (There was a complete silence for about three minutes; then the wife replied).

A: What was that date again?

DO NOT HAVE WORDS PUT IN YOUR MOUTH

Do not adopt "facts" in your replies just because the lawyer is trying to put words in your mouth with his questions. For example, if the opposing counsel asks "Isn't it true that you were in the car with the defendent at the time of the accident?" do not say "Yes" if you were not in the car. Rather say "I was not in the car at the time of the accident."

Do not accept the opposing lawyer's inferences and deductions or characterizations of time. The attorney will be stating the facts and information in his questions to put them in the best possible light for his client. You must answer the question without adopting the attorney's words; be sure to phrase your reply using your own words If you do not point out the errors contained within the question, it will be assumed you adopted those facts.*

● ● ● ● ● ● ●

Tales of the Transcript

Remember to answer the questions politely without coming off as a wise guy.

Q: You say you're innocent, yet five people swore that they saw you steal a watch.

A: ...I can produce 500 people who didn't see me steal it.

More Humor in the Court, p. 49

*Tyson, *Op. cit.*

Regarding questions of distance or time; if you do not know, do not estimate. **If you are forced to estimate, then make certain you say it is an estimate.**

● ● ● ● ● ● ●

Tales of the Transcript

Sometimes it is safe to estimate:

Q: And where was the location of the accident?

A: Approximately milepost 499.

Q: And where is milepost 499?

A: Probably between milepost 498 and 500.

DIAGRAMS OR DRAWINGS

Depending on the nature of the case and your involvement, you may be requested to diagram an intersection in an accident or a device in a product liability case. Therefore, you should, in your preparation for your deposition, anticipate such a request, practice accurately drawing what you intend to depict. Beware that such a drawing or diagram could then become an exhibit in the case and used at trial.

Your lawyer may object to your drawing a sketch or diagram as these drawings are usually not to scale and they do not accurately depict the objects or locations you are trying to describe.

● ● ● ● ● ● ●

Tales of the Transcript

Again, it is best to answer "yes" or "no" if possible.

Q: Have you ever been convicted of a felony?

A: Yes.

Q: How many?

A: One so far.

Disorder in the Court, page 29.

PREVIOUS ACCIDENTS OR INJURIES

If questioned concerning previous accidents or injuries, do not hide them; reply accurately.

●　　●　　●　　●　　●　　●　　●

Tales of the Transcript

If you do not know the answer, simply reply "I do not know." If you do not recall something, simply reply "I do not recall."

Q: Are you being selective about what you remember and what you don't remember as to the details of your previous record?

A: I don't remember.

Disorder in the Court, page 213.

DOCUMENTS/EXHIBITS

Do not testify about a document without first reading it completely prior to responding to a question concerning it. Each document introduced by the other sides' lawyer and marked as an Exhibit by the court reporter should be read top to bottom carefully even if you are extremely familiar with it. Take as much time as you require to read and understand the document. After you indicate that you have read the document, wait for a question to be asked before saying anything. Do not volunteer what you know about the document or make comments to yourself, your counsel, or others while you are reading it. **Try to keep your expressions and reaction to it neutral.**

- Beware if a document refers to another document, your lawyer should demand you review that document also.

- Do not testify about the contents of a document unless you remember the subject.

- Even if the document implies that you wrote it or got a copy of it, unless you have a definite recollection of it, do not acknowledge that you reviewed or wrote it.

- Do not hesitate to point out or dispute any inaccuracies in a document. Because certain subjects are reduced to writing it does not mean they are accurate or correct.

- You should carefully review all documents produced during discovery by the parties, so if you are asked what documents you reviewed for your deposition, you will not have to hand over just the ones you reviewed particularly related to you.

- Do not read or review any documents in preparation for your deposition without first consulting with your counsel, as one of the questions you will be asked is if you "reviewed any documents in preparation for your deposition?" If you reply "yes," you will then be asked to identify all the documents you read. However, if your lawyer gives you documents to review, you do not have to disclose what you reviewed as they will be protected by the "Attorney Work Product" privilege. Remember, however, that if your recollection has been refreshed by a document you have reviewed, you may have to identify and produce that document, even if you reviewed it with your attorney and even if it would be exempt from production but for your use of it to refresh your recollection.

• Do not review privileged or un-requested/harmful documents as then you may be compelled to produce them to the other side, unless they are provided to you by your lawyer to review.

● ● ● ● ● ● ●

FINAL QUESTIONS

At the end of your deposition, you may be asked if "you know anything else" that has not been covered on a particular topic. You should reply that you do not recall unless there is something very specific you or your lawyer thinks should be brought up.

● ● ● ● ● ● ●

Tales of the Transcript

Of course it is better to phrase your replies to put your case in the best possible light as along as it does not damage your credibility.

Q: What made you bite the police officer?

A: He stuck his arm in my mouth.

Disorder in the Court, page 167.

Typically, your own attorney will only ask you questions after the other side is finished with you, to clear up an issue that might be confusing in the record, to fill in a void or gap in the record, to make the record more consistent, to make certain a particular item is on the record, or to avoid any implication that you were not able to provide testimony on a particular subject. Also, if you make an error in reply to a question by the opposing lawyer and advise your lawyer of your error, he may try to get the correct reply on the record, although in most cases, your lawyer will have you correct your error while the opposing counsel is still examining you if that can be done.

● ● ● ● ● ● ●

Tales of the Transcript

Reply to the question and be quiet – there is no need to try to explain your answer.

Q: Officer, at this point in your own mind, did you consider him to b a suspect in the homicide?

A: No. I really did not have enough intelligence to make that decision.

Disorder in the Court, page 189.

VIDEOTAPED DEPOSITIONS

Your deposition preparation is even more critical in a videotaped deposition. Your deposition is being videotaped so it may be shown at trial. You must reply as though you are speaking to the judge or jury, not just the attorneys present at the deposition. You should face the camera when responding to questions. Do not look across the table at the questioning attorney or at your attorney.*

In a videotaped deposition overall appearance and demeanor is very important, so dress and conduct yourself appropriately.

Do not engage in distracting mannerisms, such as tapping you finger, playing with papers or rocking back and forth. Beware that your deposition is also being audio-taped. Therefore, during a videotaped deposition, a jury will be able to hear the tone of your responses. You must, therefore, behave as though you are in front of a judge or jury at all times.

Remember that at a videotaped deposition you should avoid long pauses and delays before replying. They are more obvious than they would be in a regular deposition and such delays might suggest a lack of candor or evasiveness.

● ● ● ● ● ● ●

Tales of the Transcript

A lawyer reports that one witness had obviously been told by his counsel, not just to take his time, but to count to ten before answering. Throughout the deposition, the witness's lips moved as he dutifully did so. Think what a disaster that would have been on a videotaped deposition.

*Tyson, *Op. cit.*

AFTER YOUR DEPOSITION

Chapter 3 – After Your Deposition

Once your deposition is completed, you will receive a transcribed copy of it in the form of a bound booklet to review. The transcription of your deposition usually takes from one week to three weeks. Once you receive a copy, you must review it within a set period of time. Be certain to read your deposition transcript carefully. This gives you an opportunity to correct errors in the transcript. You can correct wrong dates, misspellings, typos and related types of changes. You will need to provide a reason for each change you make. If you find other errors, call them to the attention of your lawyer. Changes must be noted on a transcript review sheet provided by the court reporter. Do not write your changes on the actual transcript. If you change your replies too much or too significantly, the other side may complain and challenge the changes at trial. If you do not sign and return the deposition transcript an unsigned one may be introduced at trial, and whatever is in it will be considered to be a true and accurate record of your deposition. Note that the other side will likely be permitted to "comment" at trial on any changes that you make to the transcript.

The time to review your deposition varies from jurisdiction to jurisdiction, but the period is usually thirty (30) days or less.

● ● ● ● ● ● ●

Tales of the Transcript

Q: And is your correct address 1845 Main?

A: Yes, it is.

Q: Do you plan on staying there for the foreseeable future?

A: Not that long.

Disorder in the Court, page 213.

CHANGES TO YOUR DEPOSITION

Any changes you make to your deposition are readily noticeable to all the parties. If you make significant changes at settlement conferences or at trial the other side can argue that your testimony is not credible. If you make too many significant changes, you can run the risk that the judge will order your deposition be resumed so the other side can ask the reasons for the changes. Therefore, it is best to be well prepared so your testimony at your deposition is as accurate and strong as possible.

● ● ● ● ● ● ●

Tales of the Transcript

Do not make a lot of changes to your deposition without reviewing them with your lawyer. A published 9th Circuit decision in *Combs v. Rockwell International* where plaintiff's counsel, without his client's consent, changed all the key deposition admissions, for the express purpose of impeding the other sides' ability to get summary judgment. Counsel even filed a declaration with the court saying, in almost these exact words, "I had to change the answers, because otherwise Rockwell would get summary judgment."

SUPPLEMENTATION

You are required to supplement your answers if, after your deposition, facts and replies provided at your deposition are proven incorrect or outdated.

Bibliography

Bergman, Paul and Albert Moore. *Nolo's Deposition Handbook*. Second Edition, 2001.

Gilman, Mary Louise. *More Humor in the Court*. Vienna, VA: National Shorthand Reporters Association, 1984.

Heileman, John. *Pride Before the Fall – The Trials of Bill Gates and the End of the Microsoft Era*. New York: Harpers Collins Publishers, 2001

Jones, Rodney R., Charles M. Sevilla, and Gerald F. Uelman. *Disorderly Conduct*. New York: W.W. Norton and Company, Inc., 1987.

Lathan, Virginia A. *The Deposition Handbook*. Chicago: Curry Publications, 2002.

Sevilla, Charles M. *Disorder in the Court*. New York: W.W. Norton & Company, Inc., 1992.

Index